The
Empath's
Empowerment
Journal

YOUR SELF-CARE COMPANION

JUDITH ORLOFF, MD

sounds true
BOULDER, COLORADO

Sounds True
Boulder, CO 80306

Published 2019

Cover design by Lisa Kerans
Book design by Karen Polaski

Printed in Canada

10 9 8 7 6 5 4 3 2 1

This book belongs to:

_____

your name here

Contact information:

_____

in case this journal gets lost

Check all that apply:

☐ I am an empath

☐ I'm a friend or relative of an empath

☐ I'm exploring whether or not I am an empath

PRIVACY WARNING

Do not read this journal without permission!

INTRODUCTION

I have always loved journals.

As a psychiatrist and an empath, I am excited to offer you *The Empath's Empowerment Journal* as a tool that inspires you to work and play with understanding your empathic nature.

Being an empath is an incredible opportunity to live with compassion, intuition, and an open heart—and it also has very real challenges, such as not absorbing other people's stress. I know what it's like to feel different and not be seen or have my sensitivities supported. Growing up, I felt like an alien and wished that a spaceship would take me to my true home.

Now I realize the great gift of being an empath and of being different. I want to impart this comforting knowing to you.

May this journal help you embody your empathic gifts more deeply and joyously. May it provide a refuge that allows you to connect to yourself and explore what it means to have healthy relationships. This journal is not meant to be simply a cerebral experience but one that is flowing, energizing, intuitive, and playful.

Make this journal your own. Be raw. Be truthful. Have fun. Take it everywhere with you to record spontaneous musings. You may also use it as a companion to my book *Thriving as an Empath*, which offers daily guidance for sensitive people. See page 163 for an index of topics that appear in both books so that you can go deeper here.

Prepare to explore. May this journal be your safe place, your friend, and your launchpad to becoming an empowered empath over a lifetime.

Judith Orloff, MD
Venice Beach, California

HOW TO USE THIS JOURNAL

1. Hold your journal close to your heart and send it love.

2. You can go through the journal topics in order or turn to random pages.

3. Follow the instructions on each page. Or ignore the instructions completely and do whatever moves you. It's your journal.

4. Let each page be an opportunity to grow more empowered as an empath.

Draw a big square.

Inside it write 5 ways that you feel
different from other people.

Draw a big bow on top of the square. Now it's a present!

How is your uniqueness a gift in your own life?
How is it a gift to the world?

I am a loving, empathic person.
I am not "too sensitive."

My sensitivity is a strength because:

I embrace my sensitivity through:

I celebrate my sensitivity by:

List 3 negative messages you received
about your sensitivity growing up.

➤ _____
_____
_____
_____
_____

➤ _____
_____
_____
_____
_____

➤ _____
_____
_____
_____
_____

Write in big, bold letters next to them:

THIS IS NOT REALITY. THIS IS NOT TRUE.

_____

_____

_____

_____

_____

_____

_____

_____

_____

_____

_____

_____

_____

_____

_____

_____

_____

I honor the gifts of my sensitivity.

My empathy is a powerful ally.

Turn to a random page. Write a love note to yourself on the margin to find later.

Do this as many
times as you like.

DRAW A BIG HEART HERE

Inside, write down things that touch your
heart. Use colored pencils or pens to draw
rays of love shining out from this heart.

What steps can I take to protect
my open, loving heart?

Do you believe you have to remove the pain of others to be a compassionate person? Why or why not?

3 **ways I express my empathy and compassion for others:**

3 ways I can hold a supportive space for someone without taking on their pain:

It is not my job to take
on the world's pain.

I respect the healing process of others without trying to fix them.

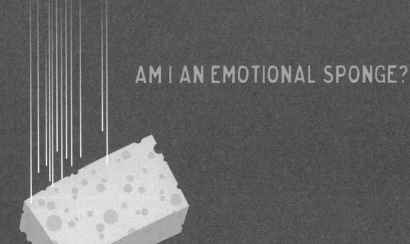

AM I AN EMOTIONAL SPONGE?

Empaths often absorb other people's emotions without realizing it. The next time you feel a change in mood or energy level after a conversation, ask yourself, "Is this emotion mine?"

List 5 ways you take on other people's emotions and stress:

1. Other peoples' anger raises my blood pressure, other peoples' stress creates stress in me.

2. Other peoples' sadness can send me into depression because I can feel it myself

3.

4.

5.

**When a loved one is stressed,
I practice these steps to center myself:**

- I say to myself, "This is their emotion, not mine."

- I find a private place and inhale
  and exhale slowly.

- With each breath, stress floats
  away and dissolves.

- All around my body I see a shield of white
  light that repels tension and negativity.

- Only positive energy can flow in
  and out past this shield.

- I come back to my loved one feeling more
  positive, protected, and balanced.

What other steps do you take to protect yourself
from absorbing the emotions of others?

Take 5 deep, conscious breaths to release stress.

Write about how this helps you.

EMPATHS NEED ALONE TIME

This pie represents 1 whole day. Color in a
pie slice that represents your ideal amount of
daily alone time. Now write a recipe for how
you can create that time for yourself.

RECIPE FOR ALONE-TIME PIE

INGREDIENTS

DIRECTIONS

Cut out and place where you can see it.

29

Solitude is for me
a fount of healing
which makes my
life worth living.

CARL JUNG

I enjoy the
peace of my own
company. I carve
out alone time
to decompress.

WHO ARE THE ENERGY DRAINERS IN MY LIFE?

3 draining encounters I have had:

1

2

3

3 kind and direct ways I can remove or protect myself from these types of situations in the future:

1

2

3

These are 3 people who make me feel good in my life:

This is how they nourish my energy:

BE MINDFUL OF YOUR ENERGY LEVEL

How does your energy feel throughout the day? Take a week to note your energy level in the morning, afternoon, and evening. Fill in the week's dates here:

__ __ / __ __ / __ __

Morning: _____

Afternoon: _____

Evening: _____

__ __ / __ __ / __ __

Morning: _____

Afternoon: _____

Evening: _____

__ __ / __ __ / __ __

Morning: _____

Afternoon: _____

Evening: _____

__ __ / __ __ / __ __

Morning: _____

Afternoon: _____

Evening: _____

__ __ / __ __ / __ __

Morning: _____

Afternoon: _____

Evening: _____

__ __ / __ __ / __ __

Morning: _____

Afternoon: _____

Evening: _____

__ __ / __ __ / __ __

Morning: _____

Afternoon: _____

Evening: _____

How can these observations help
you conserve your energy?

I listen to my intuition about activities and people who drain or nurture me. I seek out positive people and situations every day. When people are draining me, I lovingly and firmly find a way to limit or end the interaction.

It is important to protect yourself from being overwhelmed. Take these steps to center yourself through meditation:

- Sit in a comfortable position.

- Relax and soften your heart.

- Bring your attention back to the now.

- Tell yourself, "When negative thoughts intrude, I let them float by like clouds in the sky."

- Feel the rhythm of your breath.

- Let serenity permeate your being.

What other strategies do you
use to center yourself?

I recenter myself
and release stress
by going inward.
I breathe slowly and
focus on my heart.

Meditation calms
empaths. Meditate
for at least 3 minutes
and write about
your experience.

Look deep into
nature and then
you will understand
everything better.

ALBERT EINSTEIN

Nature nourishes empaths. Take your journal outside and experience the wonder of nature—even if you're in the city. Record your spontaneous thoughts or feelings. What forms of nature do you love?

Collect a small token from nature, such as a feather or leaf. Say, "Thank you!" and tape it on this page.

THE POWER
OF EARTH

It is grounding for empaths to
connect with the earth. Earthing
will energize you! Find a way to
put your hands or feet in direct
contact with the ground today.
Note how it makes you feel.

What grounded, earthy qualities do I have?

What new ones would I like to develop?

I am replenished by being in nature.
I rest in the grace of the natural world
and allow it to fill me.

The sun can strongly affect an empath's mood and energy. The summer solstice is the most light-filled day of the year. It is a good time for empaths to focus on RADIATING their inner light.

THE NEXT SUMMER SOLSTICE IS ON ___/___/___ .

What will you do to honor the life-giving power of the sun on this day? How will you let your light shine more brightly?

The winter solstice is a day of maximum darkness, inviting empaths to embrace the serenity and quiet they need.

THE NEXT WINTER SOLSTICE IS ON ___ / ___ / ___ .

How will you honor this time of inward reflection and the return of the light?

The moon's phases can strongly affect
an empath's mood and energy.

The new moon and full moon are good days
to meditate and replenish yourself.

THE NEXT NEW MOON IS ON ___/___/___ .

What fresh start can I make on this day?

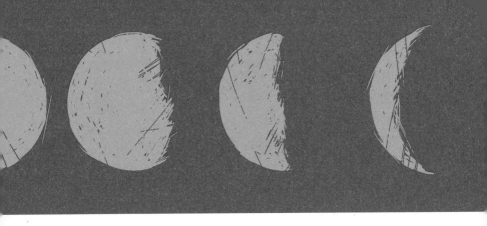

THE NEXT FULL MOON IS ON ___ / ___ / ___ .

What can I do to ground myself and also take
in the full moon's power on this day?

MOVE YOUR BODY

Physical exercise, yoga, and stretching help you release negativity and stress. List some favorite ways you can move your body and exercise.

Indoors:

Outdoors:

Alone:

With others:

Empaths need to love themselves
but may have self-doubts.

Draw or paste a picture of an angel watching
over you with a caption saying:

I LOVE YOU.
YOU ARE PERFECT JUST AS YOU ARE.

PRACTICE SELF-COMPASSION EVERY DAY

I will practice
self-compassion and
release negative
thoughts about myself.

I vow to beat myself up a
little bit less each day.

_____

Sign here

Empaths must learn to set healthy boundaries to thrive. How does it feel to set a boundary by saying no?

ME

People or situations I can say no to today:

THE POWER OF AIR

It is freeing for empaths to be in the open air, to feel spaciousness. Take a walk and notice the breeze on your skin and in your hair. Pay attention to the space around objects and people.

What open, expansive, air-like qualities do I have?

What new ones would I like to develop?

MAKE A SENSITIVITY COLLAGE

Cut out pictures or words from magazines
that celebrate your sensitivity. Include
different textures and colors that inspire you.
Make them into a collage here.

LISTEN TO YOUR INTUITION

Intuition is the still, small voice inside that tells you the truth about things. It comes through as gut feelings, "ah-ha!" experiences, dreams, knowings, and signals from your body.

What intuitions do you listen to?

I pay attention
to the messages
my body sends.

I follow my intuition's
advice and notice
the results.

We all have energy fields that extend beyond the body. Empaths can intuitively sense this.

Trace an outline of your hand or toes here.

Use colored pens or pencils to draw your energy field that extends around it.

Now close your eyes and let yourself connect to your body and your subtle energy field.

A true intuition feels compassionate or neutral.
A fear feels critical or emotionally charged.

AND FEAR?

Think of a time when your intuition was
confirmed. What did it feel like to be correct?

MY TOP 5 FEARS

(1)

(2)

(3)

(4)

(5)

For now, assume these are not accurate intuitions.
Pick 1 fear and write down what would relieve it:

Practice automatic writing to access
your intuition. Without thinking,
let your nondominant hand write
and see what messages appear.

DREAMS

Many empaths receive intuitive information from their dreams. For the next week, let your dreams guide you. Fill in the dates here and then place this journal by your bed. Every night before you go to sleep, ask a question that you would like a dream to answer. Record whatever you remember as soon as you wake up, even if it's just 1 scene.

___ ___ / ___ ___ / ___ ___

Question:

Dream:

___ ___ / ___ ___ / ___ ___

Question:

Dream:

___ ___ / ___ ___ / ___ ___

Question:

Dream:

__ __ / __ __ / __ __

Question:

Dream:

__ __ / __ __ / __ __

Question:

Dream:

__ __ / __ __ / __ __

Question:

Dream:

__ __ / __ __ / __ __

Question:

Dream:

How did your dreams help to answer your questions?

If you need more space, use any of the blank pages in this journal.

I turn to my dreams for guidance.

I trust my inner knowing.

Managing your time wisely is a secret to high energy, especially for empaths.

Name 1 daily activity you dread:

What baby steps can you take to eliminate or modify this?

Name 1 daily activity you love:

Write about how grateful you are for this:

I DESERVE TO HAVE FULFILLING WORK

These aspects of my work nourish me:

These aspects of my work drain me:

I can improve my current work experience by:

If I had my way, my work would satisfy me by:

I make space for freedom by
creating a regular daily routine.

I find a balance between
structure and spontaneity.

Empaths tend to be overly serious.
Take time to play!

If you had to obey this sign,
how would you spend your day?

I don't have to do
everything at once.

Baby steps
are golden.

It is safe to open my heart.

This is what my big, open, sensitive heart looks like:

This is what I need to feel safe enough
to open it up to others:

....
....
....
....
....
....
....
....
....
....
....
....
....
....
....
....
....

Empaths often struggle with wanting love and also wanting to be alone.

3 things I love about being on my own:

3 things I love about being in a relationship:

3 things that make being in a relationship balanced and comfortable for me:

How do you maintain your identity
while in loving relationship?

ME

**Activities I do
without my partner.**

Activities we

Fill in this diagram. Reflect on and write
about what this exercise reveals to you.

MY PARTNER

do together.

**Activities my partner
does without me.**

I maintain balance
in my relationships.

I will not lose myself.

Marry yourself!

The most important relationship
you will ever have is with you.

Create these vows to
declare your commitment.

Dear beloved

_____ ,

YOUR NAME HERE

I am present here today to unite with you in
a sacred bond, in sickness and in health.

Today, I vow to care for my own
body, mind, and spirit.

I promise to show you that I love you by:

_____

I promise to honor you by:

_____

I promise to cherish you by:

_____

With endless devotion,

_____

YOUR NAME HERE

RELEASE THE NEGATIVE VOICES OF YOUR CHILDHOOD.

**5 negative messages my parents
gave me when I was growing up:**

1.)

2.)

3.)

4.)

5.)

**Here is what I
know instead:**

I honor the gifts that my mother gave me, even as I follow my own unique path apart from hers.

It is not my job to carry
any of my mother's
emotions or burdens.

I honor the gifts that my father gave me, even as I follow my own unique path apart from his.

It is not my job to carry any of my father's emotions or burdens.

Burn some sage or sweetgrass
to clear any negativity out
of your home and out of
your mind. Collect the ash
in a dish and use it to draw
a flower with your finger:

DON'T LET YOUR OWN THOUGHTS DRAIN YOU!

What would your life be like if you never
had these thoughts again?

THE POWER OF WATER

Empaths often feel energized around water. The next time you take a bath or a shower, turn it into a ritual to cleanse yourself of toxic emotions and stress.

What flowing, water-like qualities do I have?

What new ones would I like to develop?

There are 3 kinds of business:
my business, your business,
and none of my business.

Empaths tend to overhelp others
and take on responsibilities that
are not their own. This is called
codependency. In contrast, healthy
interdependence is when you
give and receive in balanced ways.
Reflect on the difference between
these two types of relationships.

I rely on other people for:

Other people rely on me for:

I am not responsible for:

I am personally responsible for:

I will heal the codependent
patterns in my relationships.

I will find ways to foster healthy interdependence with others.

PRACTICE THE
HO'OPONOPONO PRAYER

Experience the grace of forgiveness. When you forgive, you don't change the past. You change the future. Recite this prayer by Dr. Ihaleakala Hew Len to release judgments about others or yourself:

I'm sorry

Please forgive me

I love you

Thank you

What would it be like to forgive

_____

for

_____

_____

_____ ?

How would I feel more free?

_____

_____

_____

_____

_____

_____

_____

_____

Holding onto regrets drains your energy.
List 3 regrets that you are ready to release:

1.)

2.)

3.)

How can you learn from past regrets to
prepare yourself for a better future?

I see missed opportunities
as reasons to grow.
I gratefully accept the gifts
that are offered to me now.

LET GO OF RESENTMENTS

To free yourself, write down 3 resentments
you are ready to release. Then tear this page
out of the journal and burn it or shred it.

1

2

3

THE POWER
OF FIRE

Fire helps you tap into your
passion and creativity as an
empath. Spend a day paying
attention to where you encounter
fire and heat. Fire represents
your own inner light and vitality.

Let it shine!

What passionate, fiery qualities do I have?

What new ones would I like to develop?

THE SEARCH IS OVER

Nothing to do
Nothing to be
Nothing to have
Rest in your own natural
Perfection
As is
Calling off the search

—ANN BUCK

Give up the search. Leave this page blank.
Put down this book and allow
yourself to just *be* for an hour.

I am free.

My past does not
control me.

Every day
is new.

LAUGHTER BOOSTS MY ENERGY!

5 things that make me laugh:

1.

2.

3.

4.

5.

5 THINGS ABOUT MY SENSITIVITIES I AM GRATEFUL FOR:

1.

2.

3.

4.

5.

WHO ARE THE SENSITIVE PEOPLE IN YOUR LIFE?

Ask a few other empaths to write
their names or thoughts on this page.
Feel the positive energy of community.

I AM AN EMPOWERED EMPATH

5 ways I feel empowered as an empath:

1

2

3

4

5

5 ways I want to become more empowered and grow:

1

2

3

4

5

If you could design a billboard about being an empowered empath, what would it say?

I will practice
self-soothing strategies
when I need them.

I know how to comfort
myself in trying times.

Write down 5 different self-soothing
techniques that work for you:

1

2

3

4

5

I will take time to
commune with Spirit.

I experience the
light and hope
that is within
and around me.

As an empowered empath,
I listen to my mind and my heart.

Write about a decision you are facing, giving
both your head and your heart a chance to speak.
Where do they agree? Where do they disagree?

Logical Solutions

BIG DECISION:

Intuitive Insights

I will be a positive role model for newly awakened empaths.

How can you offer simple support to a fellow empath—but not take them on as a project? What kind of mentorship feels good to you?

_____

_____

_____

_____

_____

_____

_____

I humbly embrace the
power of being sensitive.

I am a beacon of light
for myself and others.

THE
EMPOWERED
EMPATH'S
VOW

I vow to protect and honor my sensitivities.

I am excited about what my life will bring
and my ongoing learning as an empath.

I will focus on the brightness of my future
and the surprises that lie ahead.

*All is well and getting better
in every dimension!*

_____

Sign here

THESE BLANK PAGES ARE ALL YOURS

... to further explore your empath nature.

THE END . . .

Actually, there is no end.

You just keep growing

brighter and brighter.

INDEX

Use this handy index to find the pages in this journal that correspond to specific topics in *Thriving as an Empath: 365 Days of Self-Care for Sensitive People.*

ABOUT THE AUTHOR

Judith Orloff, MD, is a psychiatrist and *New York Times* bestselling author. Her books include *Thriving as an Empath: 365 Days of Self-Care for Sensitive People* (the companion to this journal) and *The Empath's Survival Guide*. Dr. Orloff specializes in treating empaths and highly sensitive people in her Los Angeles private practice. An empath herself, Dr. Orloff synthesizes the pearls of conventional medical wisdom with cutting-edge knowledge of intuition, spirituality, and energy medicine. She is also the author of *Emotional Freedom*, *Positive Energy*, and *Second Sight*. Her work has been featured on the *Today Show*; CNN; and PBS; in *USA Today*; the *New York Times*; and *O, The Oprah Magazine*; and at Google. To learn more about empaths, *The Empath's Survival Guide Online Course*, or to join Dr. Orloff's Empath Support Community on Facebook and newsletter, visit drjudithorloff.com.

ABOUT SOUNDS TRUE

Sounds True is a multimedia publisher whose mission is to inspire and support personal transformation and spiritual awakening. Founded in 1985 and located in Boulder, Colorado, we work with many of the leading spiritual teachers, thinkers, healers, and visionary artists of our time. We strive with every title to preserve the essential "living wisdom" of the author or artist. It is our goal to create products that not only provide information to a reader or listener, but that also embody the quality of a wisdom transmission.

For those seeking genuine transformation, Sounds True is your trusted partner. At SoundsTrue.com you will find a wealth of free resources to support your journey, including exclusive weekly audio interviews, free downloads, interactive learning tools, and other special savings on all our titles.

To learn more, please visit SoundsTrue.com/ freegifts or call us toll-free at 800.333.9185.